Therapy Games for Teens

200 Mindful Activities for Enhanced Coping Skills, Expression, and Self-Worth

Table of Contents

Introduction Letter to Parents

Dear Parents,

Your teenager's mental health and emotional development are important to you – or you wouldn't have picked up this book in the first place.

Teenagers are uniquely vulnerable. At this point in their life, they are looking to you for support while exploring their identity and striving for independence. Combined with natural hormonal changes, teens often face mental health challenges that can follow them into adulthood. If you are reading this book, you care about your teenager's mental health and want to support their growth.

The activities are designed as a resource, not to replace your support, but to complement it. They are also intended to give your teenager the tools they need to support their *own* mental health. We encourage you to actively engage and communicate with your teenager and participate in activities alongside them so they know you are with them on their journey.

Introduction Letter to Teen Readers

Dear Teen,

You have been given this book by somebody you trust. It does not mean you're broken!

We all need help navigating through our lives. Your struggles with school, life, relationships, and friendships are normal. This book is designed to give you tools to help you stay on an even keel, even if your grades aren't what you want them to be or the person you have a crush on won't give you the time of day.

Believe it or not, we've all been there. The activities and tips in this book have been shown to help teenagers deal with everything that, right now, seems like it might be the end of the world. Use this book to help and rely on the trusted adults in your life for advice and support.

Chapter 1: Understanding the Power of Mindfulness

Mindfulness sounds weird, but it's actually a very simple concept. So, let's start by understanding what it is and what it can do for you.

What Is Mindfulness?

Mindfulness is being aware of the moment, yourself, and your surroundings. A lot of the time, we rush from one thing to another without thinking. Think about your typical school day and how you dive from class to class, chat with your friends over lunch, and then rush home or to extra-curricular activities. You might not have time to stop.

Mindfulness is all about stopping, even if it's only for a moment, and checking in with yourself.

The Benefits of Mindfulness

Think back to the last time you played some kind of sport. If you don't know where the ball is, you can't catch it, right?

So, mindfulness starts by knowing where your personal balls are. You can't fix a problem if you don't know what it is, which also goes for your mental health.

Getting that kind of awareness is not easy, but it's well worth it. Here are some ways mindfulness can make your life better:

- It makes you less anxious. Think about how much easier exams and tests would be if you worried less about them.

- It increases your self-awareness, helping you be a better person.

- It increases your awareness of your emotions, letting you regulate them better.

- It helps you sleep better.

- It can increase your performance in sports by reducing stress and performance anxiety.

- It improves relationships by giving you better control over emotions and behaviors that can alienate your friends and family.

Mindfulness can help every single part of your life. It's not just for people who are having problems. It's for everyone. Lots of famous people swear by mindfulness meditation to help their lives and make them more successful: Emma Watson, Lady Gaga, Katy Perry, Miley Cyrus, and LeBron James are a few examples. We bet your favorite celebrity does it, too.

Mindfulness Games

Here are some exercises to improve your mindfulness:

1. Basic Walking Meditation

Walking meditation can help you improve your mindfulness.[1]

a. Choose a space 10 to 20 feet long or a quiet path.

b. Walk along the space or the path, turning at the end.

c. Focus entirely on the act of walking, on the movements that help you stay balanced.

2. Body Scan Meditation

a. Lie on your back with your legs extended, arms at your side, palms up.

b. Focus your attention on each part of your body, from your toes to your head.

c. Be aware of sensations, emotions, or thoughts associated with each part.

3. Sitting Meditation

a. Sit with your back straight, feet on the floor, and hands in your lap. Choose a chair that is not too comfortable or too uncomfortable.

b. Breathe through your nose.

c. Make a note of each sensation or thought that interrupts you, then return to your breath.

4. Paced Breathing to Reduce Anxiety

a. Inhale for four counts.

b. Exhale for seven counts.

5. Progressive Muscle Relaxation

a. Focus on a body part and then tense and relax muscles. You can do your shoulders, hands, etc.

6. 5-4-3-2-1

This is an awesome grounding exercise. Pay attention and mention out loud or internally:

a. Five things you can see

b. Four sensations you can feel

c. Three sounds you can hear

d. Two things you can smell

e. One thing you can taste.

7. Personality Tree

a. Write your values on the roots

b. Write your strengths on the trunk

c. Write your goals on the branches.

8. Raisin Meditation

a. Take a raisin (or some other small fruit)

b. Note the color

c. Feel the texture

d. Smell the raisin

e. Put the raisin in your mouth and savor the taste

f. Eat the raisin

9. Use STOP

    a. **S**tand up and breathe.

    b. **T**une into your body.

    c. **O**bserve what your body is telling you.

    d. **P**ossible: What is possible here?

10. Yawn and Stretch

Consciously yawning and stretching help you be more aware of your body.

Yawning and stretching can make you more aware of your body.[2]

11. Be Your Own Best Friend

Tell yourself the things you would tell a friend in your situation. This stops negative self-talk.

12. Mindful Cleaning

Nobody likes cleaning their messy room. But if you turn it into a mindfulness activity, it will help your mood, and it will actually get done!

13. Dancing

    a. Put on a favorite song.

    b. Dance to it with your eyes closed. Focus only on the music and how you are moving.

Dancing can help with mindfulness.[3]

14. Mantras

A mantra is simply a word or short phrase.

    a. Choose something aspirational, such as "peace" or "calm."

    b. Think about that word/mantra with each breath.

15. Box Breathing

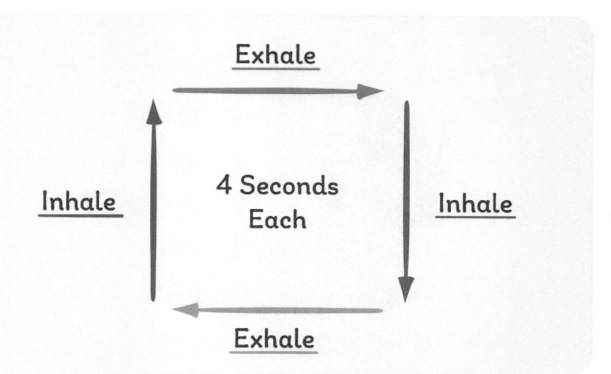

a. Inhale and envision drawing one side of a box.

b. Exhale and do the second side.

c. Inhale for the third side.

d. Exhale for the fourth side.

e. Repeat as needed.

16. Safari

a. Take a walk in a park or the woods.

b. Try to find all the animals, insects, and plants you can.

This is great to do with siblings or parents. Leave your phone at home.

17. Blowing Bubbles

a. Get some bubble solution at the dollar store, or make it with dish soap and water.

b. Blow bubbles and watch them.

Blowing bubbles can improve mindfulness.[4]

18. Mindful Cooking

a. Choose a simple, familiar meal.

b. Examine each ingredient and how they look, feel, and smell.

c. Prepare the meal with focus.

d. Eat the meal, focusing on it, with no phone or TV.

19. Three Good Things

a. Acknowledge your feelings.

b. Name three good things happening in your life. Your parents can help with this one.

20. Puzzles

Doing your favorite crossword puzzle, Sudoku, etc., without interruptions is a great mindfulness exercise.

Sudoku

Crossword

Section 2: Expressing Your Thoughts

Self-expression is really important! We all fall into the trap of thinking we should only do creative things if we happen to be good at them. That's not true. In fact, we benefit from letting ourselves be bad at things. That said, the satisfaction of learning to do something well helps our confidence.

There are a variety of creative mediums you can use, which include:

- Journaling
- Art
- Fiction
- Crafting
- Music
- Poetry

Different mediums use different parts of your brain. You will probably find one or two that help you more than others, so try them all and see what helps.

How Creativity Works with Mindfulness

Mindfulness and creativity go together. Art therapy, for example, helps people with depression and anxiety. At the same time, mindfulness helps you be more creative. Being creative then helps you express yourself, become more aware of your emotions, and develop a skill. Also, it's a lot of fun.

Creative Exercises

Here are some creative exercises that will help you be more mindful and happier.

21. Painting Kindness Stones

    a. Take a large pebble.

    b. Paint a design on it.

    c. Add an affirmative word such as "Hope," "Love," or "Family." You could also do pictures of your pets or the name of a friend – or your own name.

22. Adult Coloring Books. Coloring is *not* just for little kids. Staying within the lines requires focus, and you can pick colors to be realistic...or not.

23. Journaling. Journaling can be writing, art, or both. You could even try a photo journal. It helps you be aware of all that's happening in your life.

Journaling can help you become more aware of what's happening in your life.[5]

24. Poetry Slam

    a. Write a poem that expresses your emotions.

    b. Get together with trusted friends.

    c. Read your poems to each other with as much force as possible.

25. Playlists

Years ago, people used to make:" mix tapes." Now, we make *playlists*.

    a. Come up with a mood you want to create or a story you want to tell

    b. Put together music that supports that mood, using tracks you own or your favorite streaming service

Creating playlists depending on your mood can help you express your thoughts.[6]

26. Write a Story from a Prompt. Use a word or image as a starting point, such as "ogre" or "castle."

27. Free Association. This means writing or drawing the first things that come into your head. If stumped, you can use a prompt, such as opening a book to a random page and starting with the first line.

28. Fashion Show! Get together with friends or family and hit the catwalk in your best (or, if you prefer, the most ridiculous) outfit.

29. Write a Letter to Yourself

    a. Imagine you're an adult.

    b. Write a letter with advice to your present self. Get your parents to help with this one.

30. Collage Yourself. (*Or Mood Board, if You Prefer.*)

    a. Focus on your values and the things you find important.

    b. Collect images that show what they mean to you.

31. Write a Song. Songwriting is a great way to express yourself as it brings together music and poetry.

Songwriting can help you express yourself.[7]

32. Develop Your Photography Skills. You already have a phone (probably), and going out and taking pictures of things in your neighborhood is a lot of fun. It also helps you notice what you might not have otherwise seen.

33. Blackout Poetry (Also Called "Found Word Poetry")

    a. Take a page of a book or newspaper (you can make a photocopy).

    b. Blank out words until what's left forms a poem.

34. Origami. The ancient art of paper folding. You can find lots of patterns online to make various creatures and images.

Origami has many patterns.[8]

35. Mandalas. Another ancient art. Drawing a mandala in sand, if available, or on paper requires a lot of focus and relaxation.

36. Bag Self-Portrait

    a. Get a paper bag.

    b. Draw a self-portrait on the outside, which can be accurate or stylized.

    c. Fill the bag with items that represent you.

37. Draw Yourself as a Warrior. Or a scientist, astronaut, superhero, or whatever represents personal strength to you. This can help you feel stronger.

38. Dress as a Warrior. Making your own costume to wear can be incredibly fulfilling, and you don't need to be able to sew. You can put it together from your wardrobe or visit thrift stores.

39. Draw or Write about Things That Scare You. This can help you feel as if you're in control of the monsters.

40. Write a Fairy Tale about Yourself, with a Happy Ending That Is Personal to You

Section 3: Managing Stress and Anxiety

We all get stressed and anxious. Being a teenager can be really stressful. You have to worry about your grades, friendships, and position on a sports team. Sometimes, it feels like so many expectations are placed on you that you will never meet all of them!

Don't worry! It's normal to be stressed. In the U.S., three-quarters of high school students experience boredom, anger, fear, or stress in school. The same number are "often or always" stressed by their schoolwork.

We can't always get rid of the causes of our stress, but managing it better can help us stay healthy. If you are really stressed, there's no shame in seeking professional help. A good therapist can give you even more tools to help with your stress.

Benefits of Improved Stress Management

Managing your stress better can help you:

- Have better relationships
- Keep up with your responsibilities
- Sleep better
- Stay healthy
- Be happier overall

There are many ways to manage your stress, including going on walks in nature, talking it out with a trusted adult, making time for fun, and writing it down. Mindfulness has been shown to reduce stress and improve self-esteem and overall mental health.

Stress Management Games

Here are some activities that can help reduce your stress.

41. Deep Breathing. Paced breathing (inhale for four counts, exhale for seven counts) can help reduce anxiety in the moment. When we breathe deeply, we actually affect our body in ways that reduce stress.

42. Put Your Hands in Water

    a. Fill a bowl or go to a stream.

    b. Put your hands in the water.

    c. Focus on the water's temperature and how it feels on parts of your hand.

Putting your hand in a stream can reduce stress.[9]

43. Hold a Piece of Ice

    a. Get a chunk of ice from the freezer

    b. Hold it until it starts to melt and focus on the sensation changes that it brings.

44. Do Jumping Jacks. Jumping jacks move your entire body and are just tricky enough that they need a lot of focus.

Jumping jacks can help you focus.[10]

45. Recite a Poem, Song, or Book Passage That You Know *Really* Well. The trick here is to focus deeply on it anyway!

46. Practice Self-Kindness. Repeat compassionate phrases to yourself. Tell yourself you are strong and trying hard, and keep saying it until you believe it.

47. Use Cognitive Reframing

    a. Acknowledge your negative thoughts.

    b. Consciously turn them into positive ones. This can be hard, so don't be afraid to get help.

48. Keep a Mood Tracker

   a. Design a mood tracker that reflects your passions.

   b. Track your mood each day and pay attention to what might have affected it.

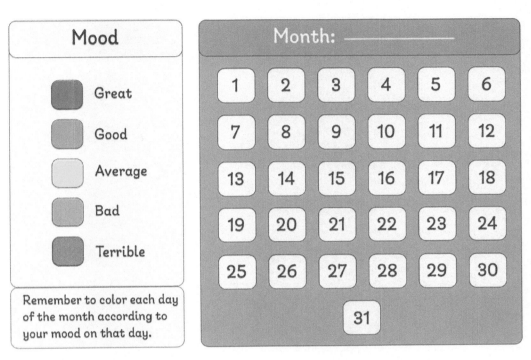

49. Anchor Breathing

   a. Imagine that you are in a place you find relaxing, such as a boat on the ocean or deep in the woods.

   b. Breathe deeply.

50. Happy Place

   a. Imagine a place where you are happy.

   b. Write down a description with as many details as possible.

   c. When stressed, visualize your happy space.

51. Throw Away Your Stress

   a. Write the things bothering you on a piece of paper.

   b. Crumple it up and throw it away. If you use rice paper (which doesn't harm wildlife), you can throw it in a river or stream and watch the water take it away.

52. Make a Gratitude Journal. Write down one thing every day that happened that was good. More than one if you want!

53. Write a Self-Forgiveness Sheet

    a. Write down your mistakes

    b. Add "I forgive myself" to each one.

54. Watch Something for Five Minutes. This can be a cloud, an insect, or your pet.

Watching clouds can relieve your stress.[11]

55. Write an Affirmation List

    a. Write down positive affirmations such as "I am strong," "This will work out," "I can be patient."

    b. Read your affirmation list when you feel stressed.

56. Fog the Mirror

    a. Hold your hand up in front of your mouth.

    b. Exhale as if deliberately fogging a mirror, making your breath audible.

57. Find a Touchstone

    a. Go to a natural place.

    b. Collect a rock, leaf, pine cone, or similar object.

    c. Touch or look at your touchstone when you feel stressed.

58. Surf Your Worries

    a. Think of a recent event that made you stressed and worried.

    b. Let the anxiety rise, and observe your sensations.

    c. Let the emotional wave crash over you.

59. The Big Shrug

When tense, our shoulders creep upwards.

    1. Sit down.

    2. Close your eyes.

    3. Tighten your shoulders up to your ears.

    4. Count to five.

    5. Drop your shoulders as low as you can.

Repeat five times.

60. Thought Flowing

    a. Sit down.

    b. Imagine your thoughts are leaves in a stream or clouds floating past.

    c. Observe each thought and then let it go.

Imagine your thoughts floating down a stream.[12]

Section 4: Building Emotional Resilience

Emotional resilience gets a bad rap. A lot of people think that it means not feeling emotions. This is not true! In fact, the last thing you want to do is try to stop feeling an emotion. When you suppress a negative emotion, such as anger, all you do is build up pressure that will eventually explode.

Instead, emotional resilience is coping with your emotions. Anger, fear, disappointment, etc., are all perfectly natural. However, if we let them control us, we have problems. Failing to control anger, for example, can alienate people and even get you into trouble with the police. Failing to control fear means you won't do things that get you outside your comfort zone and help you grow. Emotional resilience also gives you better self-esteem and vice versa.

How to Build Emotional Resilience

You can't build emotional resilience overnight, and you shouldn't try. It's an ongoing process that you will be working on your entire life. You've seen adults fail to control their temper or get upset about a small disappointment, right? We all have setbacks, and they're part of life. That includes the ones you're learning to deal with *and* setbacks while dealing with them.

Resilience is about growing and adapting to the challenges you face every day.

Emotional Resilience Exercises

Some exercises to improve emotional resilience:

61. Create Your Own Support Circle. This would be family members and friends you can rely on and trust. It might include peers and adults, a trusted teacher, an older mentor, etc.

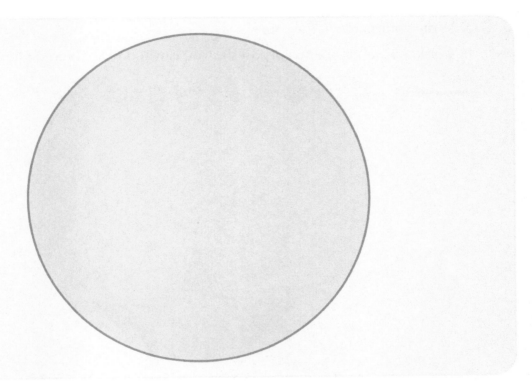

62. Practice Gratitude

    a. Write down a list of things you are grateful for, from the big ones (such as having a home) to the little things that happen every day.

    b. Use your gratitude list to remind you that the bad things aren't so bad.

63. Challenge Journaling

    a. Write down the challenges you faced that day.

    b. Write how you responded to them.

    c. Ask yourself how you could have done better and write that down.

64. Use a Coping Mantra. Come up with a phrase that helps you break the cycle of worried thoughts – such as, "I'm doing the best I can," "It's going to be okay," or "I am a strong person."

65. Tell a Different Story

    a. Write down the event that made you angry or sad.

    b. Rewrite it to have a happier interpretation.

66. Make a Purpose Star

    a. Write your name in the center.

    b. Come up with as many purposes as you can and write them on the arms.

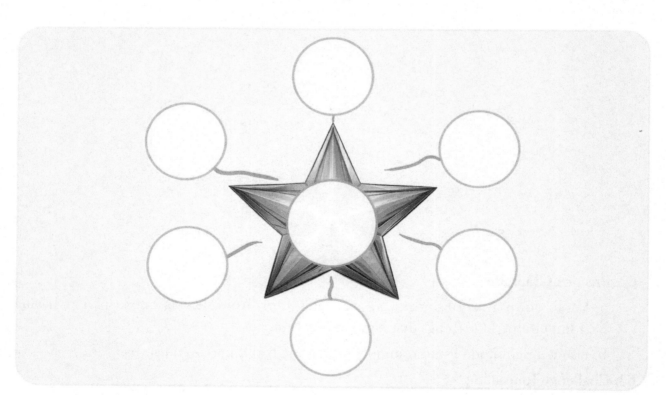

67. Collect Your Strengths

    a. Ask five people close to you to write down what they see as your top strengths.

    b. Look for ones that appear more than once.

68. Random Act of Kindness. This might be picking up something somebody dropped, paying for a stranger's coffee, etc. Choose somebody you don't know and don't expect anything back from.

69. Find Something Funny. Write down the three funniest things you've seen that day before going to bed. If you haven't seen anything, look for funny anecdotes online.

70. Practice Self-Compassion

    a. Write down the challenging event.

    b. Write down what you would tell a good friend about it.

71. Find Uniqueness. Write down the things that make you different from others. Then, reflect on them.

72. Improve Physical Resilience. List one small change you can make to improve your health, such as drinking more water or going to bed fifteen minutes earlier.

73. Write a Gratitude Letter to Somebody Who Has Helped You Out Recently. And yes, then send it to them!

Writing a letter to someone can help you build resilience.[13]

74. Reframe Thinking

    a. Write down the worst thing that could happen in the challenge you just faced.

    b. Write down the best thing.

    c. Write down what you would tell a friend.

75. It Could be Worse.
Write down three ways the challenging situation could have been worse. For example, if a friend flaked on you, think, "I could have no friends at all," "They could never come back," or "I could have nobody to talk to about this." Imagining things being worse can help instill gratitude.

76. Color a Mandala.
Don't think about what colors you use, but use the ones that feel right. This helps you slow down and relax.

77. Write and Destroy a Letter

If you're mad at somebody:

    a. Write them a letter explaining all the reasons you're angry with them.

    b. Delete it, burn it, or shred it. This helps you go through your anger rather than suppressing it. They need never know.

78. *Perfect Is the Enemy of Done* Exercise

    a. Write a story or make a piece of artwork.

    b. Don't edit, revise, or adjust it (don't do this with your homework!)

    c. Show it to somebody.

79. Name Your Feelings.
List all of the emotions you are experiencing and just say them or write them down. This helps avoid an emotional "flood" that can be hard to deal with.

80. Do a Goal Worksheet

    a. Set goals for the week and the month. Keep them achievable so you feel good when you meet them.

    b. If you fail, write down why, being sure to separate out the external factors you can't control and need to work on not worrying about.

Do a Goal Worksheet

Month _____	Goal: _____ _____	Failed? Write down why
Week 1	Goal: _____ _____	_____ _____ _____ _____ _____ _____ _____ _____
Week 2	Goal: _____ _____	
Week 3	Goal: _____ _____	
Week 4	Goal: _____ _____	

Section 5: Confidence Boosting Techniques

Do you feel confident? If your answer is some variant of "No," then that's normal. A lot of teenagers, especially girls, struggle with low self-esteem. Social media and being tied to our phones don't help. Social media encourages us to compare ourselves to our peers or, worse, to celebrities with unrealistic body types. There's also bullying and negative online feedback, such as being called "fat" by people you don't even really know. Or, worse, by people you thought were your friends.

Other things that can impact confidence are being over-scheduled, feeling pushed to be "perfect" by yourself or others, or doing things you don't enjoy and aren't good at because they look good on your college admissions essay.

Building Confidence

Confidence doesn't mean being cocky. In fact, the guy who always seems to be doing everything boldly may be hiding insecurity.

Confidence is very personal, and it involves awareness of your own abilities, trust in them, confidence in your body, etc. It takes time to build confidence, and it's a personal journey that's different for everyone. You don't need to feel jealous of someone with more confidence than you (especially as comparing yourself to others is a great way to *lose* confidence).

Instead, always compare yourself to yourself and look at where you were a few months ago for inspiration.

Confidence Building Techniques

Here are some easy techniques that can help you build confidence:

81. Power Posing

Power posing can help you boost your confidence.

For a few minutes daily, adopt a pose that feels powerful to you. Maybe put your hands on your hips like Wonder Woman or reach up to the sky to make yourself bigger.

82. Positive Self-Talk

Take some time to tell yourself how wonderful you are. If you feel worthless, tell yourself you are worthy. If you feel unloved, remind yourself of the people who love you.

83. Skill Building

Taking up a new hobby and being a beginner can actually be a great confidence booster! We learn more quickly when learning something new, which always feels like an achievement.

Taking up a new hobby, like playing an instrument, can boost your confidence.[14]

84. Goal Setting

Set achievable goals and then reward yourself when you meet them. You may want to work with your parents on this. For example, they can help you come up with rewards. Always set goals that are within your control. "I will get an A in chemistry" is not within your control. "I will hand in all of my chemistry homework on time" is a more reasonable goal.

85. Keep a Compliment Journal

    a. Whenever anyone says anything good about you, put it in the journal.

    b. When you feel like you can't do anything, reread those past compliments.

86. Self-Portrait Exercise

    a. Sketch a self-portrait.

    b. Tell yourself how wonderful it looks.

87. Core Belief Exercise

    a. Write down three negative core beliefs you have about yourself, such as "I am not attractive" or "I am not smart."

    b. Come up with reasons why they aren't true. Or have your parents or a good friend or both tell you why they aren't true.

Negative core beliefs	Reasons why they aren't true

88. Positive Word of the Day. Each day, write down a positive word that describes something you did that day, such as "Helpful," "Kind," or "Victorious."

89. Mirror Exercise

    a. Stand in front of the mirror.

    b. Come up with three things you find beautiful about yourself.

Talking to yourself in the mirror can help you see what you like about yourself.[15]

90. Give Yourself a Certificate. When you achieve something, award yourself a certificate for the achievement. Maybe it's a better grade than expected or being helpful to a friend.

91. Play a Cooperative Board Game with Your Friends. Cooperative board games encourage social interaction and reduce competition.

92. Do a Self-Appreciation Project

    a. Print out or draw the body template.

    b. Write all the good things about yourself you can think of inside the template.

    c. Have your friends and family write all the good things they notice *outside* the template.

    d. Put it somewhere you can see it.

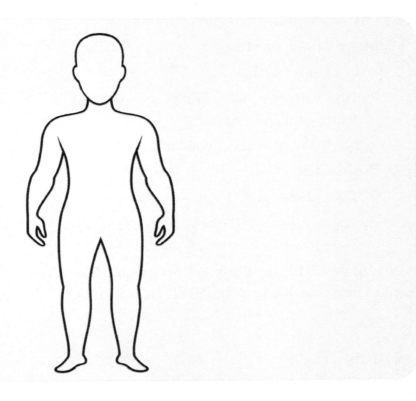

93. Build a Wall of Fame

a. Get a large corkboard.

b. Hang it in your room.

c. Attach proof of your accomplishments. This might include a list of your grades, a medal or certificate you run in sports, a printout of a note of praise, and your name badge from volunteering. Put it where you can easily see it while doing tasks such as homework.

94. Create a Mental Highlight Reel

a. Visualize the times you experience success.

b. Rerun the "reel" in your mind when feeling incompetent or lacking confidence.

95. Do Something You Are Afraid to Do. This shouldn't be something actually dangerous but think of things like approaching somebody at school who intimidates you, doing a task you aren't sure you can achieve, etc.

96. Write and Share a Story or Poem. Read a poem to your friends. Maybe enter a writing contest for teenagers.

97. Do a Social Media Purge. Go through your "friends" list and remove anyone who doesn't make you feel good about yourself.

98. Make a Book of Mistakes

    a. List your mistakes

    b. Add what you will do differently next time. If you can't think of anything, seek help from somebody you trust.

    c. Mark any "mistakes" you and your friends think came from external factors.

99. Play the Filter Game.

    a. Take photos and videos.

    b. Do silly things with them. This will remind you that perfect images on the internet or in a movie were probably altered.

100. Make a Photo Book or Scrapbook Showcasing Your Passions, Interests, and the People Most Valuable to You. Feel Free to Include Pets!

Creating a scrapbook will help you see your passions and interests more clearly.[16]

Section 6: Creating a Mindset of Growth

Think of all the adults in your life. Some of them seem stuck where they are and stuck in "can't." Others are constantly learning and taking up new hobbies at the age of 70. The first set has a fixed mindset, and the second set has a growth mindset.

Having a growth mindset means acknowledging that you will never stop learning, growing, and changing. It also means understanding that this is a good thing. Carol Dweck has been researching this for years. According to her, a fixed mindset is the belief that your intellectual ability is fixed and that if you can't do it now, you can never do it. A growth mindset is a belief that you will always be able to develop and improve your abilities.

You can probably work out which is better.

Developing a Growth Mindset

A growth mindset means seeing setbacks as temporary, learning from your mistakes (and other people's), and valuing process over outcome. For example, a fixed mindset might lead to you judging yourself by your grades, which might be affected by your mood the day you took a test, your teacher's mood the day he graded it, or how tough the teacher is. A growth mindset judges by how you achieved those grades and what you learned.

For example, "I can't draw" is an example of a fixed mindset. The alternative is, "I want to be able to draw; how do I get there?" This doesn't mean you should feel as if you have to work on things you don't want to do or don't support your goals.

Growth Mindset Exercises

101. Make and Decorate Growth Posters

    a. Take a large sheet of paper.

    b. Write your next goal on it.

    c. Make it pretty with your favorite doodles.

102. The Paper Challenge

    a. Take paper and scissors.

    b. Try to duplicate the tricky shape. Don't give up; it's not easy, and you may fail a few times.

103. Make Growth Mindset Bookmarks. If you read all the time, these are great because you'll be reminded every time you open your book.

   a. Cut a strip of paper or light cardboard.

   b. Write a phrase or Mantra that indicates growth, such as "I can learn to do this."

   c. Add a ribbon to the bottom.

   d. Laminate it if you can.

104. Research a Famous Failure

   a. Spend some time online and find a famous person who failed hard before they succeeded.

   b. Tell your family or friends about them. Good starting points are Walt Disney, Thomas Edison, and Stephen King.

105. Read Every Day. Challenge yourself to read a chapter of a book every day for a month. You will probably want to keep going! It doesn't matter what the book is – but choose one that challenges you!

Reading can help you create a growth mindset.[17]

106. Make a Vision Board. A vision board is a collage of your dreams and desires. It's images that represent what you want to do and achieve. Include things you aren't sure you *can* do.

    a. Get a corkboard.

    b. Collect and print out images that represent your desires.

    c. Put it somewhere you can easily see. Or you can do one on your computer.

107. 3-2-1 Exercise

At the end of a day or week, write down the following:

   a. Three things you have learned.

   b. Two things you want to learn.

   c. One question you still have.

108. Keep a Thought Journal. Write down a thought every day that reflects your attitude toward learning. You can spot when you are slipping into a fixed mindset. Then, take those fixed mindset thoughts and change them into growth mindset thoughts!

109. Make a Memory Jar

   a. Take a decent-sized jar.

   b. Every time you achieve something, write it on a slip of paper, then put it in the jar.

   c. Each week, open the jar and read through your accomplishments.

Filling up a memory jar can give you a sense of accomplishment.[18]

110. Success Iceberg Exercise

a. Write a goal at the top.

b. Write your failures and setbacks below the water line.

c. When you succeed, write that above the water line at the top.

d. Keep it as a reminder that you will almost always fail multiple times before succeeding.

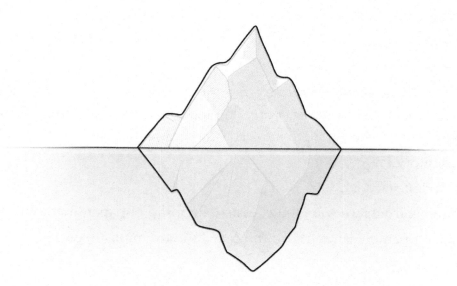

111. Write a Success List

a. Write down different ways to achieve success.

b. Add different definitions of success (hint: It's not always making the most money). This is even more fun if you brainstorm it with somebody else.

112. Use the "Brains Get Stronger" Mantra. Repeat it to yourself a few times. Your brain is actually developing a lot right now, and just like a muscle, if you use it, it gets bigger and better.

113. Play the Yet Game

a. Make a statement such as "I don't know" or "I can't."

b. Add yet to the end.

114. Flip the Flop

a. Take a piece of paper.

b. Write a mistake on one side.

c. Think of an opportunity that mistake created and write it on the other.

115. Try a New Thing. This can be as simple as that video game you've wanted to play but think is too hard for you. Let yourself be a beginner.

116. Moonshot Goal

a. Think of something you really want but are convinced you will never achieve, such as writing a book or getting into your preferred college. Take it as far as you want.

b. Write it down.

c. Think of things you can do that will be steps toward your moonshot goal.

117. Do an Already Learned Worksheet

a. Create a worksheet with sections for when you were a baby, a toddler, a child, a teenager, and also an adult.

b. Write down what you have already learned, and yes, this includes how to walk.

c. In the adult section, write down things you hope to learn in the future.

Already Learned Worksheet

Age	Already Learned
Baby	
Toddler	
Child	
Teen	
Adult	

118. Do Error Analysis

    a. Write down a mistake you made.

    b. Write down why you made the mistake.

    c. Write down how you can keep it from happening again.

119. Analyze a Fictional Character

    a. Take a book you love.

    b. Ask yourself if the protagonist has a fixed or growth mindset.

    c. Ask yourself when they change from one to the other.

120. Research Somebody Else's Success. Don't choose a famous person from a famous family. Look at somebody closer to home to see how they worked for their success.

Section 7: Building Social Skills: The Essentials

Without social skills, you won't succeed in life. You won't be able to succeed in a job. More than that, you won't be able to hold stable relationships. Think about how you get on (or don't) with your peers.

It's easy to think that you are the way you are socially, but remember the last chapter! You can improve your social skills, even if you're shy. It just takes time and practice. You don't have to turn into a bubbly extrovert, but you *can* learn to interact better with others.

What Are Social Skills?

We bandy the phrase social skills around a lot but don't often define it. Here are some examples of social skills:

- **Verbal Communication**. Being able to talk clearly and explain what you want to say.

- **Nonverbal Communication**. Making eye contact and controlling your body language.

- **Active Listening**. Being focused on the person you are talking to.

- **Empathy**. Developing an understanding of what other people are feeling.

Yes, people often start with different aptitudes for these skills, but everyone can improve them.

Games to Improve Social Skills

A lot of the activities in this chapter require more than one person. Enlist a sibling, a friend, another family member, etc. You can play these games with your entire family if you want!

121. Use a Conversation Starter

This doesn't mean the weather. Look online, and you can find lots of lists of conversation starters, but consider things like "What have you achieved lately?" "What do you do to relax?" "What book (or movie or TV show) are you reading/enjoying right now?"

122. Role Play

Put yourself in a scenario and practice it with your friends. You can also use this to practice difficult situations, such as finding out you weren't invited to a party or asking somebody out.

123. Conversation Jenga

    a. Get a game of Jenga.

    b. Write a conversation starter question on each block.

    c. As you play, answer the question on the block.

Conversation Jenga can boost your social skills.[19]

124. Charades

It's a classic, but a game of charades helps you practice nonverbal communication and makes everyone laugh.

125. Emotions Uno

    a. Get an Uno set

    b. Make each color in the game stand for an emotion.

    c. At the start of the game, when you play a card, mention a time you felt that emotion.

    d. After ten minutes, switch to a way you dealt with the emotion.

126. Do a Debate

Pick a fun topic and challenge each other. Choose topics that don't create actual anger for you, such as which fictional character would win in a fight.

127. Play Ball

This doesn't have to be an organized game, but any kind of team game requires physical and nonverbal communication.

Playing a sport, like basketball, can improve nonverbal communication.[20]

128. Play Devil's Advocate

 a. Have a debate.

 b. Switch sides, so you have to argue a point with which you don't agree. Choose light-hearted topics for this.

129. Improvised Stories

 a. Each chooses three objects.

 b. Give them to the player on your right.

 c. That player then has to include those objects in a short improvised story that they tell right then.

 d. Repeat until everyone has had a turn.

130. Perspective Photos

a. Take your phone and a simple object.

b. Take pictures of it from your perspective, from an ant's perspective, from a giraffe's perspective. Use editing tools if you want!

c. Show them to your friends and have them guess the perspective used.

131. Take an Art or Museum Tour with Your Friends. Choose some exhibits. Discuss them. If getting together is hard, many museums and galleries do virtual tours, which can be easier.

132. Social Interaction Observation

a. Observe an interaction between two or more people.

b. Write down what you might have done differently. You can do this at school or use a TV show or movie.

133. Round-Robin Stories

a. Tell one sentence of a story.

b. The player on your right then tells the next sentence.

c. Repeat until you have a complete story (or can't stop laughing).

134. Sing Together. Singing together encourages cooperation, helps you get empathy, and is a lot of fun.

Singing as a group can be a lot of fun.[21]

135. Do an Escape Room. If there's an escape room in your area, go with your friends or family. It's a great way to learn to really work together.

136. Play Two Truths and a Lie. Each player says three things about themselves. Two are true, and one is not. The rest of the group has to guess which one is the lie.

137. Practice Saying No

    a. Have a friend pretend to be a really pushy salesperson.

    b. Keep telling them no.

    c. Switch roles.

138. Play Spot the Mistake. One player talks about a familiar topic but makes three or four deliberate mistakes. The rest of the group has to identify the mistakes. Let everyone have a turn.

139. The Tossing Game

    a. Get a *soft* ball (this is not dodgeball).

    b. Toss the ball to somebody else and say a word.

    c. Have them toss the ball to a third person.

    d. Their "victim" must say a *related* word. For example, if the first player says brick, the second might say house. If you say an unrelated word, you're out.

140. 500 Years Ago. One person imagines they are a time traveler from 500 years ago. The other has to explain something to them in words they can understand.

Section 8: Meditation and Visualization

People have been meditating for a very long time. As far as we know, meditation first started in India and is described in *Vedic* texts from thousands of years ago. It likely started well before it was written down!

It's come to refer to many techniques, but the overall purpose is still to get in touch with your inner self. Meditation is really good for you. Especially when starting out, you need to make a quiet place to meditate. Set aside a corner of your room that's clutter-free and generally has an even temperature. You can use a seat, get a cushion, and sit on the floor. The most important thing is to have a place where you feel like meditating!

Benefits of Meditation

As mentioned, meditation is really good for your health. In fact, meditation has been shown to:

- Reduce stress and anxiety.
- Improve your mood.
- Help you sleep.
- Reduce pain, such as aching muscles from sports.
- Improve memory and recall.
- Increase efficiency in your brain, meaning you can do things faster.
- Reduce blood pressure and heart rate.
- Improve blood flow to the brain.

Meditation gets even better as you get older, so getting in the habit now sets you up for a long life!

Meditation Techniques

Meditation can be really hard to start with. Don't try to just sit there and empty your mind. That's like trying to empty a bucket resting on its side in a creek; it will just fill up again. Here are some simple techniques to get you going:

141. Body Scan Meditation

Body scan pose.

    a. Lie or sit down.

    b. Focus on your body, starting with your toes and working up to the head. Focus on each body part and notice all sensations.

142. Guided Visualization

Guided visualization means taking a mental journey. It's great for beginners because you're focusing *on* something specific. Imagine walking along a beach, through the woods, or along a mountain trail.

143. Loving Kindness Meditation

    a. Imagine a close friend or loved one is sitting opposite you

    b. Imagine you are connected to them by a white light between your hearts.

    c. Focus on the feelings you have for them

    d. Say, "May I be well, happy, and peaceful."

    e. Say, "May you be well, happy, and peaceful."

    f. Repeat a few times.

144. Labyrinth Meditation

Your community may have a labyrinth. If not, you can make a small one by setting objects on the ground in a spiral. Walk the labyrinth from the outside to the inside and back, focusing on the sensation of walking. Let your thoughts wash over you.

145. Diaphragm Breathing

A lot of us breathe in our upper chest. Breathing from the belly helps us get more air.

    a. Sit or lie on your back.

    b. Rest your hands on your belly, just below the navel.

    c. Breathe in and focus on swelling your belly like a balloon.

    d. Breathe out and let your belly sink toward your spine.

146. Concentration Meditation

Focusing on a candle flame can help with concentration meditation.[22]

a. Look at an object or listen to a repetitive sound. Candle flames are great (but watch out for your fire safety).

b. Every time your mind wanders, refocus on the chosen object.

147. Mantra Meditation

a. Choose a word or sound that includes the classic "ohm."

b. Repeat the word or sound.

148. Bead or Counting Meditation

Rosaries can be used for counting meditation.[23]

a. Get a bead necklace.

b. Count the beads and move them through your hands, focusing on them. (Rosaries are a form of bead meditation).

149. Clean Room Visualization

a. Imagine that your space is completely clean and free from clutter.

b. Focus on how it feels.

150. Shower Meditation

When you take your shower, that's a great opportunity to get in some deep breathing. Focus on how the water feels on your skin or the fragrance of your chosen soap.

151. Yoga

Yoga can help you clear your mind.[24]

You don't necessarily have to take a class; there are a lot of yoga videos out there. Yoga involves conscious postures that help clear your mind and also has the advantage of making you more flexible.

152. Reflection

a. Read a poem you like.

b. Then, spend a few minutes simply reflecting on it in silence.

153. Alternate Nostril Breathing

a. Hold your left nostril down with your left thumb.

b. Inhale through your right nostril.

c. Hold your right nostril down with your left index figure.

d. Hold your breath.

e. Release the left nostril and exhale.

f. Change sides and repeat.

154. 100-Breaths Technique

This one's easy. Just count each of your breaths to a hundred. Make sure you only count exhales.

155. Make an Energy Ball

    a. Rub your palms together.

    b. Feel the sensation of tingling and heat.

    c. Pull your hands apart with palms facing together.

    d. Move them closer and further apart and play with that feeling of connection.

156. Sound Bath

This isn't a time to choose your favorite angsty pop song. Instead, choose classical music, ambient sounds, etc. Choose music without vocals. Close your eyes and let yourself exist in the sound.

157. Noting Meditation

This means using an anchor such as a candle or sound but being careful to note all of your stray thoughts. Label each thought as it arises. This can be combined with other techniques.

158. Who Am I Meditation

This means sitting and asking yourself, "Who am I?" without attempting to answer that question. Insights may come from your subconscious.

159. Laughter Meditation

Laughter meditation can relax you.[25]

Laughter is great medicine. In this form of meditation, you intentionally start to laugh.

    a. Take a few deep breaths.

    b. Smile

    c. Laugh for a few minutes

    d. Stop laughing

    e. Sit in silence for a couple of minutes.

160. Forest Bathing

Forest bathing can be done in any natural setting.[26]

You don't need a forest; any natural place will do! This Japanese practice means just going out into a natural setting, turning off your phone, and moving slowly while taking deep breaths.

Section 9: Mind and Body Connection

"It's all in your head." Has anyone ever said this to you when you're not feeling well? Our minds and our bodies are strongly connected. A physical ailment can make us depressed, and stress and depression can make us physically ill.

When we're stressed, our adrenal glands release adrenaline and noradrenaline into our bodies, preparing us to fight, take flight, or freeze. Our bodies also release cortisol. If the "threat" continues, then elevated levels of these hormones cause problems with our immune system and increased inflammation. You're more likely to get a cold if you're stressed.

Taking care of your mind helps you take care of your body. Doctors sometimes refer people to therapists to help with this. Physical health affects our mood...imagine you break your wrist and can't play sports for a while. That's not going to make you happy!

Nurturing Your Mental and Physical Health

A lot of people, especially younger people, think they don't have time for their mental health. You need to make time! Being mentally and physically healthy means you will get tasks done faster (have more free time), get them done better (have better grades), and have a consistently better mood.

Everything in this book is, to some degree, about getting mentally healthier, but now we're going to address it more directly.

Tips for Better Health

Here are some exercises and tips to nurture your mind-body connection and improve your health.

161. Cut down on junk food and treats. Don't give them up altogether; that tends to make you binge. Instead of eating sweets every day, try having designated "Sweetie Days."

162. Switch up your lunch sandwich. If you pack a sandwich for lunch, switch out your white bread for whole-wheat bread. Add tomatoes and lettuce, spinach, or another green.

Eating a sandwich can improve your health.[27]

163. Reduce soda/pop. Don't switch to diet drinks, which have been shown to increase cravings. Go for flavored water instead. Cut out energy drinks; they're really bad for you.

164. Always eat breakfast. People who skip breakfast tend to weigh more than those who don't.

165. Challenge your friends to a jump rope or hula hoop contest. Or some other simple physical activity.

Simple physical activities like using a can slightly improve your health.[28]

166. Have a scavenger hunt on foot or on bikes. This exercises the mind and the body at the same time.

167. Eat fruit instead of candy. The natural sugar in fruit is better for you.

168. Challenge your friends to a step challenge. If you all have phones that can count your steps or fitness bands, you can set a challenge for a period of time, say a week, and see who can do the most steps.

169. Turn the volume down. Keep the volume on your phone to less than 70% of the max if using earphones.

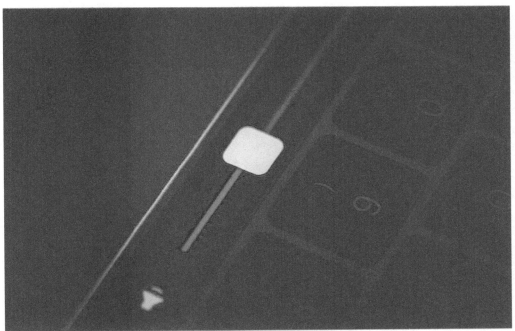

Keep the volume low if using earphones.[29]

170. Keep a regular sleep schedule. Set a bedtime and stick to it, even on weekends.

171. Avoid caffeine in the evenings. This isn't just for teenagers; it's for everyone. Caffeine late at night can keep you from sleeping.

172. Put your phone down an hour before bedtime. Reading a physical book is a great alternative. Screens interfere with your brain, producing sleep hormones. *Turn your phone off at night.*

173. Say no to alcohol and drugs. It's very tempting to try them, especially alcohol, marijuana, and tobacco. However, they're not good for you when your brain is still developing (and not great for adults, either).

174. Practice mindful eating. This means not eating while watching TV or doing homework. Focus on just eating and eat your food slowly.

175. Make fruit water for you and your family. Take a water pitcher and fill it, then add slices of fruit...lemon and lime work well, as does cucumber. Or you can use berries. It's easy and delicious.

176. Improve your posture. A simple exercise that people have been doing for a long time is to walk around with a book on your head. Challenge your friends to see who can do it for the longest.

177. Schedule time for things you love. Put it in writing so you don't forget. If you're doing your obligations all the time, you will experience "burnout" and potentially get ill.

178. Wear sunscreen every time you go outside for an extended period, especially if you have fair skin. Dark-skinned teenagers need it, too, though.

179. Pick up an active hobby or sport. Doing an active thing you love kills two birds with one stone.

Section 10: Setting a Roadmap for the Future

This book is intended as your starting point. You may find some exercises in it more useful than others. Everyone's different; what works for you might not work for others.

Try them; they may spark ideas for other ways to move forward. Ultimately, only you can decide what you most need to stay healthy and happy.

You need a clear direction in life for the future, and hopefully, this book can help you find one. You need goals.

SMART Goals

SMART goals were invented for businesses, but they also work for life! A smart goal is:

- **S**pecific
- **M**easurable
- **A**chievable
- **R**elevant
- **T**ime-bound

You might have an overall goal of starting your own successful business, but that won't work as a SMART goal because it's not time-bound. At the same level, getting straight As is also not a SMART goal because you might not be able to control all the factors that give you your grades, making it impossible.

A really good example of a SMART goal would be "I am going to eat breakfast every day next month." It's specific (tight), measurable (you can check off that you ate breakfast), achievable, relevant (supports your health), and time-bound. After next month, you will have a habit of eating breakfast.

Another example is, "I will read three books this month."

A longer-term SMART goal might be "I'm going to apply to ten colleges." This has a natural deadline. You can't control whether you get in, but you can do things that make it more likely.

You need to be adaptable and reassess your goals. Things change in your life, and things change in you. The career you thought you wanted when you were twelve might not be what you want at sixteen. (Or thirty). Take charge of your future!

Activities to Help You Plan Your Future

Some activities to help you get in the habit of planning and setting goals:

180. Vision Boards

Yes, these have been mentioned before, but that's because they're so good. Set up your vision board with images of what you want to achieve and put it where you can see it.

181. Make a Journal Jar

    a. Brainstorm with your parents or your friends to write down a long list of prompts, such as "What habits would you like to change or develop?" or "Make a bucket list."

    b. Put them in a jar.

    c. Pull one out at intervals and write on it.

182. Make a Wheel of Success

    a. Choose a goal, such as being good enough for the track team.

    b. Identify the performance attributes you need.

    c. Score where you are now.

    d. Score where you need to be. Use it to identify where you need to focus.

The Wheel of Success

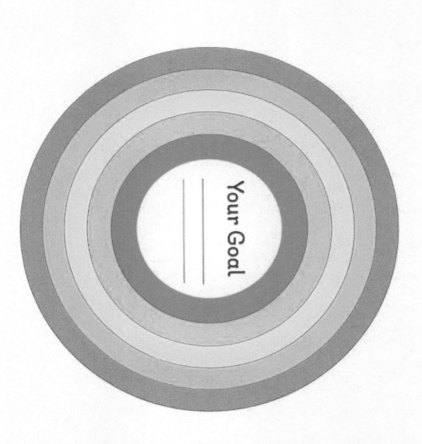

Far From
Your Goal

Close To
Your Goal

Your Goal
_____
_____

183. Make a Task List for Each Goal

    a. Break a goal down into smaller tasks

    b. Write them on a piece of paper.

    c. Check them off as they're completed. Be flexible; you may find you need to add or remove tasks.

    d. If you're feeling discouraged, look at what you already did.

Make a Task List for Each Goal

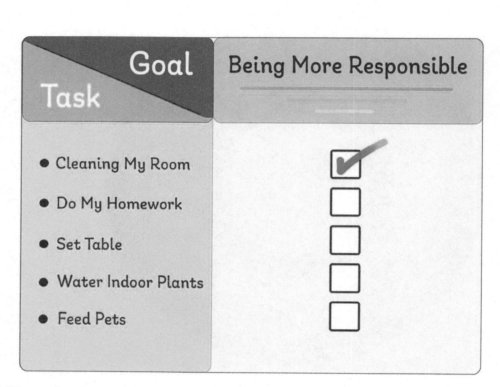

184. Use Your Goal as a Mantra. When you wake up, say your most important goal three times.

185. Make a Bucket List

Creating a bucket list can motivate you.[30]

This is a list of things you want to do or achieve in your life. It might include places you want to travel to, having kids, activities you want to engage in, etc. Good examples might be "Visit Rome," "Go bungee jumping," or "Make a pollinator garden." Not all of them will be achievable yet, and you'll keep adding items.

186. Set Rewards

Small rewards for completing each task help keep you motivated. You may want to enlist your parents here. Stickers are a great reward for small tasks. For a larger goal, maybe you can get your parents to take you somewhere fun or set up a celebration with friends.

187. Make a Past Goals Folder

For each goal, write on a sheet of paper:

    a. What the goal was.

    b. If you achieved it.

    c. Why *did* you achieve it/why *didn't* you achieve it?

    d. What the obstacles were.

188. Set Aside Time for Things That Are *Not* Part of Your Goals

If you focus on goals all the time, you can get depressed and feel as if you aren't "allowed" to relax and have fun.

189. Record the Process

For example, if you are trying to improve your running time, keep a record of your times. Then, you can look at how they have improved. If your goal is to improve your writing, looking at how bad your journal entries were a year ago can help.

190. Mirror Your Goals

Stick your goal to the bathroom mirror so you see it every time you go in there. If this would cause confusion, another great place is above your bed, where you'll see it when you get up.

191. Journal Your Wishes

a. Whenever you think or say "I wish," put it in your journal.

b. Look through your wishes to see if you can turn any of them into goals.

192. Find a Goal Buddy

This doesn't have to be somebody with the same goal, but it helps if it's a friend with a similar goal. If your goal is to work out four times a week, a friend who works with you can help.

193. Ask Your Parents or Your Buddy to Grade You on Your Goals

Strive to reach an A.

194. Set Up a "Goal Club" with Your Friends Where You Share Goals and Encourage Each Other

Don't invite anyone who is prone to criticizing everyone.

195. Clean Your Desk

Keeping your desk clean can declutter your mind.[31]

This might not seem related, but your mind gets cluttered if the space you work in is cluttered. Before doing homework, spend a few minutes removing everything irrelevant.

196. Write an Intentions List

At the start of the day, write down everything you intend to do that day. It feels good to check things off!

197. Make an Eisenhower Matrix

This is a four-square matrix that allows you to prioritize tasks as important, not important, urgent, and not urgent. Remember that fun is important too!

Make an Eisenhower Matrix

Important	Not Important

Urgent	Not Urgent

198. Use a Calendar or Planner

A calendar can help you track your progress.[32]

This helps you track everything you must do by a certain time, such as homework or things you promised a friend.

199. Take Time to Do Nothing

This is the last tip for a reason. We tend to over-schedule our lives. Sometimes, it's good to do absolutely nothing.

200. Fortune Wheel

Get a piece of cardboard paper and draw a circle on it. Divide the circle into sections and write down various goals of yours. Stick a pointer in the middle and design your wheel with colors and stickers to make it fun to use. This fortune wheel of goals can be a fun and stimulating way to choose a goal to work on when you're not sure which goal to work toward first.

Thank You Message

Thank you for buying and reading this book. More than that, thank you for committing to personal growth.

The world needs young people with grit and courage; even taking the first steps toward improving your life proves you have just that! Your future is bright.

This book is a starting point. It's a nudge in the right direction. The rest is up to you. We invite you to stay connected and to share your progress with us and each other.

Thank you for being you!

Check out another book in the series

References

(N.d.-a). ApA.org. https://www.apA.org/topics/mindfulness

(N.d.-b). Research.com. https://research.com/education/student-stress-statistics

(N.d.-c). ApA.org. https://www.apA.org/topics/children/stress

(N.d.-d). Psychologicalscience.org. https://www.psychologicalscience.org/observer/dweck-growth-mindsets

Can mindfulness exercises help me? (2022, October 11). Mayo Clinic. https://www.mayocliniC.org/healthy-lifestyle/consumer-health/in-depth/mindfulness-exercises/art-20046356

Courtney E. Ackerman, M. A. (2017, February 3). 25 fun mindfulness activities for children & teens (+tips!). Positivepsychology.com. https://positivepsychology.com/mindfulness-for-children-kids-activities/

Henriksen, D., Richardson, C., & Shack, K. (2020). Mindfulness and creativity: Implications for thinking and learning. Thinking Skills and Creativity, 37 (100689), 100689. https://doi.org/10.1016/j.tsC.2020.100689

Hu, J., Zhang, J., Hu, L., Yu, H., & Xu, J. (2021). Art therapy: A complementary treatment for mental disorders. Frontiers in Psychology, 12. https://doi.org/10.3389/fpsyg.2021.686005

Koutamanis, M., Vossen, H. G. M., & Valkenburg, P. M. (2015). Adolescents' comments in social media: Why do adolescents receive negative feedback and who is most at risk? Computers in Human Behavior, 53, 486–494. https://doi.org/10.1016/j.chB.2015.07.016

Mindfulness for kids. (2020, June 11). Mindful; Mindful Communications & Such PBC. https://www.mindful.org/mindfulness-for-kids/

On, W. (2020, November 10). How does stress affect the immune system? UMMS Health. https://health.umms.org/2020/11/10/stress-immune-system/

Raypole, C. (2019, May 24). Grounding techniques: Exercises for anxiety, PTSD, and more. Healthline. https://www.healthline.com/health/grounding-techniques

Sharma, H. (2015). Meditation: Process and effects. Ayu, 36(3), 233–237. https://doi.org/10.4103/0974-8520.182756

Surzykiewicz, J., Skalski, S. B., Sołbut, A., Rutkowski, S., & Konaszewski, K. (2022). Resilience and regulation of emotions in adolescents: Serial mediation analysis through self-esteem and the perceived social support. International Journal of Environmental Research and Public Health, 19(13), 8007. https://doi.org/10.3390/ijerph19138007

Take charge of your health: A guide for teenagers. (2023, February 27). National Institute of Diabetes and Digestive and Kidney Diseases; NIDDK – National Institute of Diabetes and Digestive and Kidney Diseases. https://www.niddk.nih.gov/health-information/weight-management/take-charge-health-guide-teenagers

Tan, L., & Martin, G. (2015). Taming the adolescent mind: a randomised controlled trial examining clinical efficacy of an adolescent mindfulness-based group programme. Child and Adolescent Mental Health, 20(1), 49–55. https://doi.org/10.1111/camh.12057

Image Sources

1 https://unsplash.com/photos/ljoCgjs63SM?utm_source=unsplash&utm_medium=referral&utm_content=creditShareLink

2 https://www.pexels.com/photo/photo-of-yawning-man-with-his-hands-up-and-eyes-closed-sitting-at-a-table-with-his-laptop-3760538/

3 https://www.pexels.com/photo/people-inside-room-12312/

4 https://www.pexels.com/photo/woman-in-white-coat-blowing-bubbles-5849026/

5 https://unsplash.com/photos/xcvXS6wDCAY?utm_source=unsplash&utm_medium=referral&utm_content=creditShareLink

6 https://unsplash.com/photos/4p0C_OiXNiM?utm_source=unsplash&utm_medium=referral&utm_content=creditShareLink

7 https://unsplash.com/photos/MlhJNEUQpBs?utm_source=unsplash&utm_medium=referral&utm_content=creditShareLink

8 https://unsplash.com/photos/Av7Nkvc49ag?utm_source=unsplash&utm_medium=referral&utm_content=creditShareLink

9 https://unsplash.com/photos/StdafGIT520?utm_source=unsplash&utm_medium=referral&utm_content=creditShareLink

10 https://unsplash.com/photos/fOS2IMOzsDA?utm_source=unsplash&utm_medium=referral&utm_content=creditShareLink

11 https://unsplash.com/photos/v9bnfMCyKbg?utm_source=unsplash&utm_medium=referral&utm_content=creditShareLink

12 https://unsplash.com/photos/jYzIgpgWgPo?utm_source=unsplash&utm_medium=referral&utm_content=creditShareLink

13 https://unsplash.com/photos/xmddEHyCisc?utm_source=unsplash&utm_medium=referral&utm_content=creditShareLink

14 https://unsplash.com/photos/4qnhBQv4qcg?utm_source=unsplash&utm_medium=referral&utm_content=creditShareLink

15 https://unsplash.com/photos/bbjmFMdWYfw?utm_source=unsplash&utm_medium=referral&utm_content=creditShareLink

16 https://www.pexels.com/photo/scrapbook-on-white-textile-3115623/

17 https://www.pexels.com/photo/photo-of-woman-wearing-beige-jumpsuit-3120864/

18 https://unsplash.com/photos/M6dAnUgiOlQ?utm_source=unsplash&utm_medium=referral&utm_content=creditShareLink

19 https://unsplash.com/photos/CqX6IhVj2TI?utm_source=unsplash&utm_medium=referral&utm_content=creditShareLink

20 https://www.pexels.com/photo/man-doing-jump-shot-1905009/

21 https://www.pexels.com/photo/group-of-friends-singing-while-sitting-on-beach-sand-7149158/

22 https://unsplash.com/photos/7GPnPHRksDE?utm_source=unsplash&utm_medium=referral&utm_content=creditShareLink

23 https://www.pexels.com/photo/close-up-shot-of-a-person-holding-a-green-beaded-necklace-8164518/

24 https://www.pexels.com/photo/photo-of-women-stretching-together-4056723/

25 https://unsplash.com/photos/khewjy5l4Zo?utm_source=unsplash&utm_medium=referral&utm_content=creditShareLink

26 https://unsplash.com/photos/sp-p7uuT0tw?utm_source=unsplash&utm_medium=referral&utm_content=creditShareLink

[27] *https://www.pexels.com/photo/a-bacon-and-egg-sandwich-over-a-wooden-box-6529599/*

[28] *https://unsplash.com/photos/mrY3CX8kL0w?utm_source=unsplash&utm_medium=referral&utm_content=creditShareLink*

[29] *https://unsplash.com/photos/QJssnBZfqmQ?utm_source=unsplash&utm_medium=referral&utm_content=creditShareLink*

[30] *https://unsplash.com/photos/R4sP8_Bq0Bw?utm_source=unsplash&utm_medium=referral&utm_content=creditShareLink*

[31] *https://unsplash.com/photos/zNRITe8NPqY?utm_source=unsplash&utm_medium=referral&utm_content=creditShareLink*

[32] *https://unsplash.com/photos/jqxB3C0YNG0?utm_source=unsplash&utm_medium=referral&utm_content=creditShareLink*

Printed in Great Britain
by Amazon

57007845R00046